Even a tiny spark of rebellion...

...can ignite a
blazing inferno.

THE VISUAL GUIDE

WRITTEN BY
ADAM BRAY

CONTENTS

FOREWORD

The first time I ever saw *Star Wars: A New Hope*, I was amazed at the images I saw on screen. I had never seen anything like it before, and it left a great impression on me. I started studying the look of the *Star Wars* universe, and the first way I did that was to read *The Empire Strikes Back Sketchbook* and *The Return of the Jedi Sketchbook* by Joe Johnston and Nilo Rodis-Jamero.

Years later, I continued that exploration and education when I began working on *Star Wars: The Clone Wars* telling stories right alongside George Lucas. It was a fascinating experience to learn how George saw the world he created, what he thought made it work, and what didn't. Everything had a purpose—every color, every shape, was relating something to the audience. Working on *The Clone Wars* was like receiving a Master's Education in *Star Wars*, and when the show ended it was time to move forward and begin a new *Star Wars* project in the post George Lucas era.

Star Wars Rebels is the first major release in an exciting new era of storytelling at Lucasfilm. To maintain the look and feel of *Star Wars*, we have brought along many of the experienced artists and production staff who worked and learned their craft directly from George Lucas. It's the responsibility of this team to keep the spirit of *Star Wars* alive, to move it forward for a new generation of fans around the world.

This visual guide to *Star Wars Rebels* reminds me of the books I used to read when I was first learning about the *Star Wars* universe. It is my hope that the images, descriptions, and details within these pages inspire a new generation of fans to dream of visiting this beloved galaxy, and imagine their own characters, their own stories, and what might be, a long time ago in a galaxy far, far away....

The Force will be with you, always.

Dave Filoni
Executive Producer

INTRODUCTION

It is a dark time. The noble Jedi are gone, and with them, the Galactic Republic itself. Where peace and justice once reigned, fear and oppression now hold sway. The Empire and its evil ruler stand triumphant over a conquered galaxy. Few dare hope for a future when they will be free once again.

TIMELINE

All dates on Lothal are measured LY (Lothal Year)—however, the origins of the Lothal calendar are lost in the mists of time.

3245 LY

INVASION OF NABOO
The evil Senator Palpatine begins his plan of galactic domination, secretly causing the downfall of the Republic's leader.

WHO WERE THE JEDI?

The Jedi Order were noble peacekeepers. They used a mysterious energy known as the Force to protect the Galactic Republic.

3255 LY

BATTLE OF GEONOSIS
(Clone Wars begin)
Palpatine, now leader of the Republic himself, provokes a galactic civil war as an excuse to seize more power.

3258 LY

ORDER 66
(Clone Wars end)
Palpatine has the Jedi Order destroyed and the Jedi wiped out.

EMPIRE IS FOUNDED
Palpatine declares himself Emperor of the Galactic Empire.

3272 LY

EZRA BRIDGER MEETS THE REBELS
A young orphan boy on Lothal encounters the crew of the space freighter *Ghost*.

THE EMPIRE

Fourteen years ago, the evil Chancellor Palpatine declared himself Emperor, and twisted the Old Republic into a brutal Galactic Empire. Now the Imperial Senate grows weaker, and control of the galaxy passes to the Emperor's ruthless military and corrupt planetary governors. The ever-expanding Empire seizes entire worlds and strips their resources to fuel its military machine.

THE REBELS

On the planet Lothal, a small group of rebels have banded together to resist the rule of the evil Empire. Struggling in isolation, they carry out missions against Imperial targets as opportunities arise. They must fight for freedom against incredible odds and menacing new enemies.

EZRA BRIDGER
A lone wolf and street-smart orphan who has found a new family.

SABINE WREN
A free-spirited teenager from Mandalore with an artistic flair.

CHOPPER (C1-10P)
The resourceful astromech droid who speaks his mind.

KANAN JARRUS

The gunslinger Jedi with a hidden past.

ZEB ORRELIOS

A brawny warrior who fights for the weak.

HERA SYNDULLA

The inspiring and caring ace pilot from Ryloth.

LOTHAL

Lothal is a frontier world, settled in the time of the Republic. The Empire came to Lothal not only to exploit its rich mineral wealth, but also to establish a new hyperspace route, expanding ever farther across the galaxy.

The plains

Lothal is covered by pleasant prairies and vast savannahs, broken by tall rock formations and long mountain ranges.

Farmhouse

Comms tower

Mining complex

Vanishing farms

Agriculture was the main industry on Lothal before the Imperial occupation. Small family farms are not as common in the landscape as they once were, and farmland is being destroyed.

Shallow seas

IMPERIAL OCCUPATION

Enormous factories manufacture weapons, TIE fighters, and other vehicles where farms once stood. These factories now pollute Lothal's skies and waterways, and vast mines tear the planet's resources from the ground.

Savannah

Temperate climate

Transportation routes

The road network leads from the capital to outlying towns, farms, factories, and mines. It is closely monitored by Imperial TIE fighters and AT-DP walkers.

Capital City

Capital City is the center of industry, commerce, and government on Lothal. It is also entirely under the control of the Imperial authorities, led by Planetary Governor Arihnda Pryce.

THE IMPERIAL OCCUPATION

The Empire has absolute power over Lothal. Thousands of soldiers and their awesome military machinery stand ready to strike any threat to Imperial authority. Hardship has become part of daily life on the planet.

Ruling by fear

Citizens prefer to avoid run-ins with Imperial troops—and the corruption, trouble, and suffering that they bring. Street vendors have learned to bribe the patrols that pass by their stalls

Imperial troops have little respect for "Loth-rats"— Lothal citizens.

The Imperial forces have been attacked several times.

questions later.

TIE fighters dock
on Imperial airfields
all over Lothal.

Imperial bases

The Empire's presence on Lothal
is especially strong. Military bases
have been built across the planet,
protecting factories and other
Imperial interests from attack.

Fighting back

There has been an increase in
attacks against Imperial forces on
Lothal lately. As unrest increases,
the ever-watchful Empire prepares
to send reinforcements.

Explosions are
now common
in Capital City.

CAPITAL CITY

The tall, white skyscrapers and blackened factories of Capital City sprawl between the grasslands and Lothal's seas. The city is a contrast of landscape and architecture, and of rich and poor.

Polluted sky

City outskirts

Imperial Command Center

Security tower

Mineral refineries

Sea port

Oppressed people

High taxes make life in Capital City miserable and expensive. This has created a thriving black market. Corrupt Imperial officials demand protection money from Lothal citizens, who sell meager goods or work like slaves in the mines and factories.

Rich and poor

At first, Lothal's population was excited when the Empire arrived. Industry tycoons, wealthy landowners, corrupt politicians, mining companies, and those with military connections all profited from deals struck with the Empire. Luxury speeders started to appear on the streets, but the average citizen saw little benefit.

Lothal architecture

The rounded, white towers of Capital City closely resemble those of Cloud City on the planet Bespin, another mining metropolis.

Government tower

Poorer residential area

Luxury residences

INDUSTRIAL CITY

Using locally mined crystals, gems, and minerals, Lothal's workers build TIE fighters, walkers, and blasters. Smoke and toxic gases rise from factory chimneys, covering the city with ash and dust. A garrison of Imperial troops stands by to make sure rebels don't interfere.

Grim alleyways

Gangsters and smugglers operate in the capital's shadows, where illegal goods are sold and corrupt Imperials prey on the weak.

Stormtrooper surveillance

Imperial stormtroopers regularly patrol the city's neighborhoods. They report their findings to Commandant Aresko and Taskmaster Grint, who in turn answer to Imperial Agent Kallus and Planetary Governor Arihnda Pryce.

EZRA BRIDGER

Ezra is a survivor. His parents, Mira and Ephraim Bridger, disappeared when he was seven years old. Ezra, now almost 15, lives on the streets of Lothal as an orphan, stealing to survive. His world, however, changes forever when he meets the rebels.

Force-sensitive kid

The Force is a mysterious energy that some beings can harness. Ezra has lightning-fast reflexes, thanks to a Force-fuelled ability to see things just before they happen. But has no idea that he is special until he meets Kanan, leader of the rebels.

STREET-SMART ORPHAN

When Ezra first meets the crew of the *Ghost*, he asks "Why should I risk my life for a bunch of strangers?" At first Ezra is reluctant to join them, yet he realizes that this path could give him purpose—and a new "family."

DID YOU KNOW?

Ezra's backpack is full of gadgets, including a wrench, flashlight, droid arm, and a holo-disk.

Ezra's tower

Ezra has a hideout in an abandoned communications tower. It is here that he keeps his impressive collection of Imperial helmets.

Protective
gloves

Backpack
full of stolen
gadgets

Energy
slingshot

DATA FILE

SPECIES: Human
AGE: 14
HOMEWORLD: Lothal
EQUIPMENT: Energy slingshot,
Imperial helmet collection,
backpack, lightsaber

A GREATER DESTINY?

Ezra had no future on the streets
of Lothal, and now he is excited
to learn the ways of the Jedi
from Kanan. He is not the most
patient student, which lands
him in big trouble sometimes!
The Force is strong in Ezra–he
has the potential to become a
powerful Jedi if he works hard.

Comlink

Knee pads
for slides
and crawls

Rookie rebel

For many years Ezra has had to look
after only himself–whatever it takes.
Putting other people before himself, and
working as part of a team, will take some
getting used to.

"Well, that was fun."

Ezra

KANAN JARRUS

Kanan is the Jedi leader of the small rebel crew. This witty gunslinger has been in hiding for years, but the struggle against the Empire means that it is getting harder for Kanan to stay out of sight.

RELUCTANT JEDI

Kanan followed Jedi Master Obi-Wan Kenobi's instruction that all Jedi should go into hiding from the Empire. He is careful not to use his Jedi abilities in public, in case he is spotted by Imperials. There is no academy for rebel leaders, however, and to survive, Kanan must tap into those old Jedi qualities of bravery, honor, and perseverance.

Protective arm guard

Gunslinger blaster

Kanan still wears his Jedi boots

Armored kneepad

Rebel leader

As a team leader, Kanan needs the crew of the *Ghost* as much as they need him. He relies heavily on Hera for support. Zeb is an ever-faithful friend to Kanan, and he is fond of Sabine and Ezra, too.

DATA FILE
SPECIES: Human
AGE: 28
HOMEWORLD: Coruscant
SPECIAL EQUIPMENT: Lightsaber, DL-18 blaster

Haunted by the past

Kanan is a survivor of "Order 66"–the moment when the Jedi were branded as traitors by the Emperor and slaughtered by his army. Kanan does not like to talk about his past, but now he must face it.

Reassembled lightsaber

Utility belt

Learning to teach

Kanan was only 14 years old when the Jedi were wiped out, and he never completed his Jedi training. He is self-conscious about this and hesitates to train Ezra. In taking on this new role however, Kanan reclaims his own journey from student to Jedi Master.

THE GENERAL

Kanan lost everything with the rise of the Empire and fall of the Jedi. For a while, his only aim in life was survival. Hera persuaded Kanan to join her to fight for a lost way of life.

Legs braced in parry position

Scrounged shin armor

"Having a laser sword doesn't make you a Jedi."

Kanan

HERA SYNDULLA

Hera is perhaps the most caring rebel in Kanan's motley band. She knows how to bring out the best in others, making her a valuable asset among the young and inexperienced team. Without her, their fragile rebellion would very quickly fall apart.

FREEDOM FIGHTER

Hera's homeworld—Ryloth—had a large resistance movement led by the freedom fighter Cham Syndulla, but eventually the planet fell to the Empire. The history of Ryloth inspires Hera's fight for freedom on Lothal.

Flying skills

Hera is an ace pilot. She has flown the *Ghost* through countless sticky situations, and she is a great shot with the ship's laser cannons. She has destroyed more Imperial ships than anyone else in the crew.

THE *GHOST*

Hera is both the owner and pilot of the *Ghost*, which means she is the captain of the ship. When the other rebels are on board, they have to do what she says.

Hera and Kanan

Hera has a special bond with Kanan. They have been working together ever since they met on the planet Gorse six years ago, when Hera convinced Kanan to fight against the Empire.

BACK-SEAT DRIVER

Hera inspires others to tap into strengths and talents that they didn't even know they had. Though she has the qualities of a natural leader, for now she remains happily in the background. While others go on missions, she waits behind as their getaway driver.

Blurrg-1120 blaster

DATA FILE

SPECIES: Twi'lek
AGE: 24
HOMEWORLD: Ryloth
EQUIPMENT: The *Ghost*, Blurrg-1120 holdout blaster

Pilot goggles

Lekku (head-tails)

DID YOU KNOW?

When Kanan first met Hera, she was already a first-rate starship pilot.

"We're out of here!"
Hera

SABINE WREN

Sabine is the weapons and explosives expert of the crew. She is tough, artistic, highly independent, and out to score big for the rebellion. Her don't-tread-on-me attitude is rooted in her Mandalorian heritage, though her teenage defiance contributes too.

A FREE SPIRIT

Sabine never questions her own motives for fighting the Empire. She simply loves the excitement and the adventure. Sabine is always ready to put herself in the middle of the action.

Graffiti artist

Sabine always seems to have an airbrush or other art supplies stashed in her gear. Her revolutionary graffiti can be found on walls, Imperial vehicles, or even on stormtrooper helmets!

Striking saboteur

Sabine is fond of explosions and creates them with artistic flair. They usually feature bright colors and shapes, making sure the mark of the rebels is clear for all to see.

Mandalorian Equipment

Targeting rangefinder

Macrobinocular viewplate

Sabine wears a traditional Mandalorian helmet and carries two WESTAR-35 blasters. She has painted all of them in brightly colored designs. Notorious bounty hunters prefer Mando gear too, which makes stormtroopers nervous when they see it!

DATA FILE

SPECIES: Human
AGE: 16
HOMEWORLD: Mandalore
EQUIPMENT: Mandalorian helmet, twin WESTAR-35 blaster pistols, airbrush and art supplies, explosives

Short hair is suited to wearing helmets

Anooba insignia (Anoobas are beasts found across the Outer Rim)

THE LOYAL MANDO

Though strong-willed and independent, Sabine appreciates her relationships aboard the *Ghost*. Sabine looks up to Kanan and Hera, and thinks of Zeb as an older brother, but she decides to ignore Ezra's awkward attraction to her.

Comlink

WESTAR-35 blaster

DID YOU KNOW?

The starbird painted on Sabine's chest is her own calling-card and a symbol for the rebel group.

Comfortable clothing for easy movement

"This is gonna be fun. Very fun."

Sabine

CHOPPER

Stubborn, self-centered, and eccentric... they just don't make astromechs like Chopper (C1-10P) any more. Chopper is so old that he is mostly made of second-hand parts. He is also grumpy, but his resourcefulness makes him an essential member of the crew.

AN UNLIKELY HERO

Chopper's logic-circuits may be faulty, but he's no dummy. In addition to being the ship's mechanic, he is a great actor. Chopper often helps the crew as a lookout or by distracting Imperials.

A GRUMPY ASTROMECH

Chopper is the opposite of loyal modern astromechs like the R2 series. He is independent, wisecracking, and doesn't care what others think about him. Chopper would rather be pulling pranks on crewmates or playing a game of holochess than doing menial tasks aboard the *Ghost*.

Fixing the *Ghost*

Chopper has protected his job among the crew by customizing the *Ghost*'s systems. He has made so many modifications that he is now the only one who can keep the ship running.

Ezra and Chopper

The only thing that Chopper does seem to appreciate is a fellow prankster with a similar sarcastic sense of humor. Of all the crew, Ezra is the most up-to-the-task, resulting in endless prank wars between the two.

DATA FILE

CLASS: Astromech droid
MANUFACTURER: Unknown
EQUIPMENT: Three grasping arms, computer probe, booster rocket, electroshock prod

Handy droid

Chopper has tons of gadgets. Like all astromechs, he has an extendable probe to interface with computer systems, navigate starships, and open doors. As a C1 model, Chopper also has three mechanical arms to manipulate objects like levers, handles, and blasters.

Slightly battered paintwork

Mechanical arm

Mismatched leg cowling

Extendable probe reaches out from here

DID YOU KNOW?

Chopper has an electroshock prod to shock his enemies. It is his favorite feature.

Booster rocket

"BLEEP BLOOP BEE-EEP!" Chopper

ZEB ORRELIOS

Garazeb "Zeb" Orrelios is a sensitive yet grouchy hulk who is more likely to punch first and ask questions later. This muscle-bound rebel shouts insults with a gruff, booming voice and loves going head-to-head with Imperial stormtroopers.

Bo-rifle (in combat staff mode)

Facial hair— an important status symbol for a Lasat

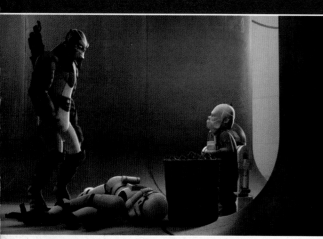

Protecting the weak

Zeb's encounters with the Empire on Lasan makes him sympathetic to the suffering of others at the hands of stormtroopers. He even refuses to use the Empire's own T-7 disrupter weapons against them, having witnessed their brutality firsthand.

Prehensile toes

DATA FILE

SPECIES: Lasat
AGE: 39 (human equivalent)
HOMEWORLD: Lasan
SPECIAL EQUIPMENT: Bo-rifle

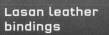
Lasan leather
bindings

Lasat combat training

As a former member of the Honor Guard of Lasan, Zeb is the only rebel with military training. Stormtroopers are no match for Zeb, and he loves nothing more than knocking a squad of them around!

BRAWN AND BRAINS

Zeb is brawny and boisterous, but not at all brainless. He speaks his mind, though not always as tactfully as he should. Zeb also has a tendency to act before thinking things through, which leads to a lot of brawls with Imperials—not that he minds!

FIGHTING FOR JUSTICE

The Empire devastated Zeb's home planet of Lasan and brutally wiped out nearly all of his people. Zeb's traumatic past motivates him to fight for freedom, and to end the Empire's tyranny once and for all.

Muscular
legs

DID YOU KNOW?

Lasats' legs enable them to run faster, jump higher, and move more quietly than a human.

"It's possible I may be a little late." Zeb

BO-RIFLES

Bo-rifles are a unique weapon used exclusively by the Lasan Honor Guard. They have a long tradition in Lasat culture. Since the destruction of Lasan by the Empire, bo-rifles are rarely seen anywhere in the galaxy. Much like a Jedi's lightsaber, they are a symbol of a dying age.

Symbol of Lasan

The Lasan bo-rifle is Zeb's signature weapon. This powerful blaster rifle is heavy and durable but it also has a jolting surprise. A bo-rifle quickly transforms into an electrified fighting staff—the perfect weapon for Zeb to pummel a squad of "bucket-heads" (stormtroopers)!

Activation sequence

Rifle systems activated

1. Collapsed mode

Collapsed for easy carrying

2. Rifle mode

Blaster trigger

Dual handles allow for powerful blows

3. Bo-staff mode

Long bo-shaft

Electromagnetic pulse generator tip

4. Bo-staff mode (activated)

Handle bar

Fighting staffs

Bo-rifles that turn into fighting staffs are a unique design, but staff weapons are found across the galaxy. IG-100 MagnaGuard droids carried electrostaffs during the Clone Wars, and the Emperor's Royal Guard use terrifying staffs known as force pikes.

Shocking power

Bo-rifle tips emit electromagnetic pulses that can stun even armored opponents. They are versatile weapons for a violent age. Zeb enjoys using his as both a club and an electric prod.

DATA FILE

MANUFACTURER: Lasan-Malamut Firearms Corporation
CLASS: Lasan Honor Guard AB-75 bo-rifle
DIMENSIONS: Rifle mode 0.13 x 0.32 x 1.01 m (0.43 x 1.50 x 3.3 ft), bo-staff mode 0.13 x 0.23 x 2.47 m (0.43 x 0.75 x 8.10 ft)

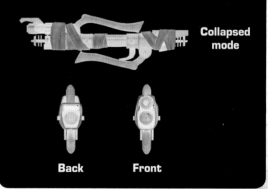

Collapsed mode

Back

Front

Decorative support straps

Blaster rifle barrel

Pulse field

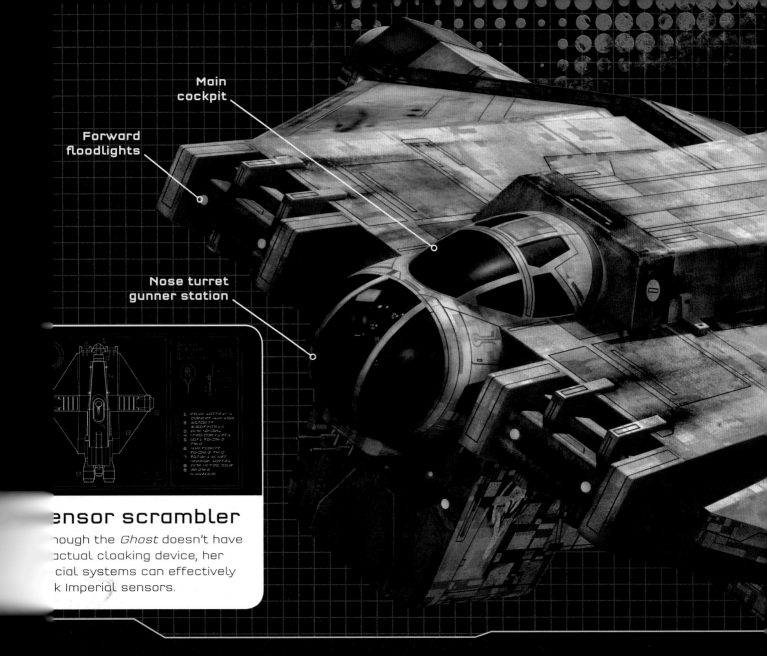

Main cockpit

Forward floodlights

Nose turret gunner station

ensor scrambler

hough the *Ghost* doesn't have ctual cloaking device, her cial systems can effectively k Imperial sensors.

THE *GHOST*

The *Ghost* is home, transporter, getaway vehicle, and battleship for the rebel crew, named because of her amazing ability to sneak past Imperial sensors undetected. The *Ghost* is made even more versatile with an additional secondary shuttle, the *Phantom*.

Hera's ship

The *Ghost* belongs to Hera, so she is understandably protective of the ship when things get out of control. If Zeb and Ezra get too rowdy, she sends them on errands to get them off the *Ghost*.

Dorsal laser cannon turret

Heavy weapons

The *Ghost* has had some close calls with Imperial Star Destroyers. TIE fighters, however, are no match for the ship's handy 360-degree dorsal laser cannon turret.

Engine assembly

Main cargo hold

DATA FILE

MANUFACTURER: Corellian Engineering Corporation
CLASS: Modified VCX-100 light freighter
DIMENSIONS: 43.9 x 34.2 x 14.5 m (144 x 112.2 x 47.5 ft)
ARMAMENT: 1 dorsal laser turret, 2 forward laser cannons, 2 rear laser cannons

Side

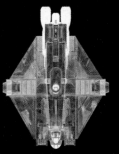

Top

Front

Secret rebel base

The *Ghost* serves as a home base for the rebel crew, and it is always on the move. Sometimes the *Ghost* docks in friendly ports, like Old Jho's Pit Stop. Other times the crew park in secluded spots out in Lothal's wilderness.

"This is my ship you're wrecking!"

HERA SYNDULLA

INSIDE THE *GHOST*

The *Ghost* wasn't built for comfort, but it provides a roomy home base for the rebel crew. As well as the cockpit and two laser turrets, there are also four staterooms, a common room, cargo bay, and galley.

Pilot controls and targeting systems

Forward turret

Weapon controls

The *Ghost* has an advanced targeting system. When a gunner isn't available to man the laser turret below the cockpit, the forward laser cannons can be aimed and fired by the pilot.

Dorsal turret

The turret on top of the *Ghost* is the only 360-degree set of laser cannons on the ship. This makes it the most important station during a TIE fighter attack. It is reached via a long ladder from the central corridor.

Strap yourself in!

The *Ghost* is a fast ship—she has outrun Imperial starships, not just the local bulk cruisers. The ship's hyperdrive has helped the crew escape from Imperial entanglements on more occasions than they can count.

Co-pilot controls and diagnostics

Passenger area

The ship's common area is the social section of the ship where the crew can lounge around and discuss missions, or play a game of Dejarik (holographic chess). Sabine has added a personal touch with some posters and graffiti.

Chopper's ship?

Though the ship belongs to Hera, sometimes Chopper seems to have a better handle on things, particularly in a crisis.

THE *PHANTOM*

The *Phantom* is the *Ghost*'s secondary shuttle craft. It is a fully armed starfighter and makes the *Ghost* unique among freighters of its class. At the front is a single-seat cockpit, with a small passenger and cargo section located behind.

Dorsal laser turret

Wraparound wing brace and cargo compartments

Phantom docked nose-first

Ghost **Rear view**

Docking position

The *Phantom* docks at the rear of the *Ghost*, just above the engines, where it adds an additional seating area to the larger ship. It can be docked nose-first, or rear-first when it can also act as the *Ghost*'s third gun emplacement.

"On my way, Spectre-5."

HERA SYNDULLA

Short-range fighter

Unlike the *Ghost*, the *Phantom* doesn't have a hyperdrive, so it is limited to short-range missions. It must return to the *Ghost* to refuel.

DATA FILE

MANUFACTURER: Corellian Engineering Corporation
CLASS: Short-range Corellian shuttle fighter
DIMENSIONS: 3.2 x 4.3 x 11.6 m (10.5 x 14.1 x 38 ft)
ARMAMENT: 1 Taim & Bak MS-2B twin laser cannon, 1 Taim & Bak KX4 dorsal laser turret

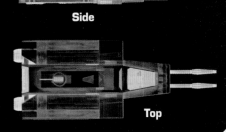

Front **Side** **Rear** **Top**

Stylized sando aqua monster

Hinged cockpit canopy

Forward laser cannons

Magnetic flashback suppressors

Unfolded wings

When one ship becomes two

The *Phantom* is ideal for making supply runs or for situations that require smaller ships to quietly sneak through Imperial space. The crew must remember to refuel the ship however, or someone could be left stranded in enemy territory.

The *Phantom*

The big guns

The *Phantom* is heavily armed for such a small craft, making it both a capable mini-transport ship and a formidable starfighter. Whether the *Phantom* is flying solo or docked at the back of the *Ghost*, TIE fighters targeted by it don't stand a chance.

LIGHTSABERS

Lightsabers are the traditional weapons of Jedi Knights. Using a lightsaber effectively requires lots of patience and intensive training. Once mastered, however, they are very powerful.

KANAN'S LIGHTSABER

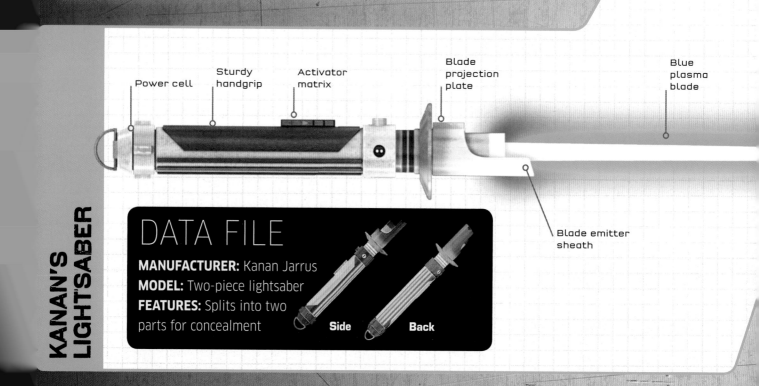

Power cell

Sturdy handgrip

Activator matrix

Blade projection plate

Blue plasma blade

Blade emitter sheath

DATA FILE

MANUFACTURER: Kanan Jarrus
MODEL: Two-piece lightsaber
FEATURES: Splits into two parts for concealment

Side   Back

EZRA'S LIGHTSABER

Padawan's prototype

Ezra's lightsaber is a unique design, a product of a less civilized age. No Jedi of the old Order would have ever considered building a blaster into their lightsaber handle. For Ezra, though, survival is more important than tradition.

Secret possession

Kanan has hidden his identity for nearly 15 years. He keeps his lightsaber disassembled in a secret compartment on board the *Ghost*. Every time he uses it, he makes himself a target for the Empire.

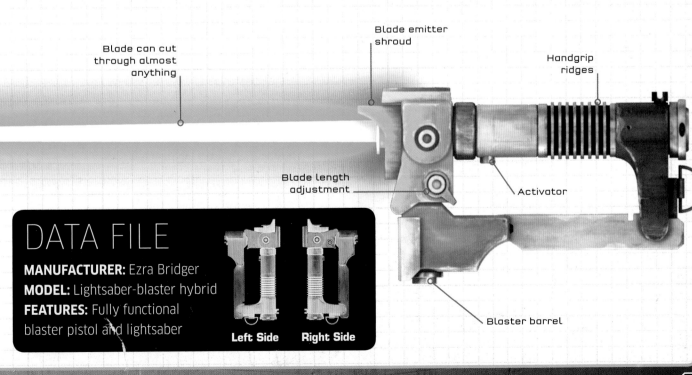

Blade can cut through almost anything

Blade emitter shroud

Handgrip ridges

Blade length adjustment

Activator

Blaster barrel

DATA FILE

MANUFACTURER: Ezra Bridger
MODEL: Lightsaber-blaster hybrid
FEATURES: Fully functional blaster pistol and lightsaber

Left Side   Right Side

REBEL BLASTERS

There is no match for a good blaster at a rebel's side. The choice of blaster also says a lot about the owner, whether they are a Jedi-in-hiding, or a Mandalorian warrior with an artistic streak.

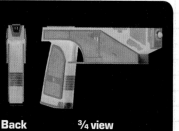

Precision barrel

Cooling unit

SABINE'S BLASTERS

DATA FILE

MANUFACTURER: Concordian Crescent Technologies
MODEL: WESTAR-35
FEATURES: Reliable, rapid-fire burst mode

Back **¾ view**

KANAN'S BLASTER

DATA FILE

MANUFACTURER: BlasTech Industries
MODEL: DL-18
FEATURES: Inexpensive, reliable, easily customized

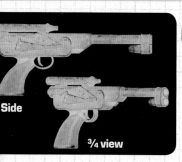

Side

¾ view

HERA'S BLASTER

Gas and power cell cartridge

Sight

Secondary blaster barrel

Primary blaster barrel

Ergonomic grip handle

"Lekku" trigger

Blurrg-1120 holdout blaster

Hera's blaster was created by a company associated with Twi'lek freedom fighters during the Clone Wars, and is now a symbol of resistance. It is named after a creature native to Ryloth.

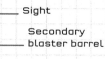

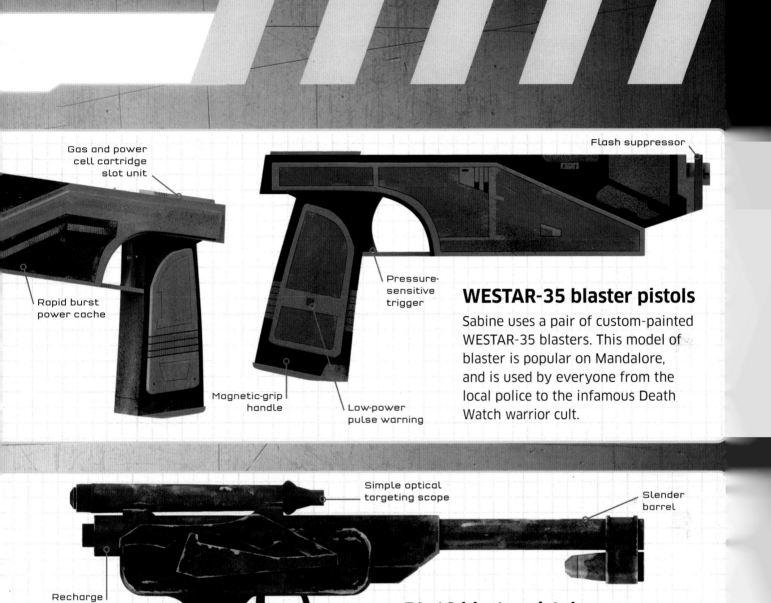

Gas and power
cell cartridge
slot unit

Flash suppressor

Rapid burst
power cache

Pressure-
sensitive
trigger

WESTAR-35 blaster pistols

Sabine uses a pair of custom-painted
WESTAR-35 blasters. This model of
blaster is popular on Mandalore,
and is used by everyone from the
local police to the infamous Death
Watch warrior cult.

Magnetic-grip
handle

Low-power
pulse warning

Simple optical
targeting scope

Slender
barrel

Recharge
valve

DL-18 blaster pistol

Although it is not a traditional weapon of the
Jedi, Kanan favors a DL-18 much of the time,
since drawing his lightsaber would attract
unwanted Imperial attention. The DL-18 is
widespread across the galaxy, particularly
among smugglers and bounty hunters.

Sensitive
trigger

Dewback skin
handle grip

DATA FILE

MANUFACTURER: Eirriss
Ryloth Defence Tech
MODEL: Blurrg-1120
FEATURES: 9 firing modes, including
single and double shot

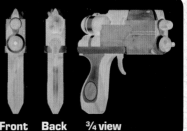

Front   Back   ¾ view

IMPERIAL ARMY

Stormtroopers are the foot soldiers of the Empire. They replaced the clone armies of the Republic, and now serve throughout the galaxy. Underneath their distinctive white battle armor are loyal Imperial citizens—though not necessarily very bright ones.

Visual processor

Stormtrooper commander pauldron

Trained troops

The original soldiers of the Grand Army of the Republic were clones. Stormtroopers, however, are mostly naturally born men and women, trained in brutal Imperial academies.

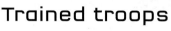

Broadband communications antenna

Vocalizer

Misuse of power

Whether through fear or loyalty, stormtroopers commit some terrible acts in the name of the Emperor. Many also use their power for personal gain, taking advantage of the weak and the helpless along the way.

STORMTROOPER EQUIPMENT

Stormtroopers regularly have their equipment upgraded with the latest technology. This advanced armor can be worn across the galaxy in extreme environments, allowing stormtroopers to fight for the Empire in deserts, forests, icy wastelands, or in space.

STORMTROOPER ARMOR

Reinforced helmet

Plastoid composite armor

Environmental controls

Combat helmets

Far more than mere "bucket-heads," stormtrooper helmets offer protection in both battle and hazardous conditions. The helmet's systems help troopers see in darkness, glare, and smoke.

Audio pick-up

Artificial air-supply hose

Plastoid protection

The overlapping plates of stormtrooper armor allow for mobility while also providing maximum protection. The plastoid material disperses the energy from a blaster hit, preventing or reducing injury to the wearer.

Sniper position knee protector plate

Positive-grip boots

Body glove

Range-finder sight

Cooling fins

Setting adjust

Trigger with safety catch

Magnatomic adhesion grip

E-11 blaster rifle

Lethal force

Stormtroopers carry an E-11 BlasTech standard Imperial sidearm or BlasTech DLT-20A laser rifle. They also have one BlasTech N-20 Baradium-core thermal detonator on the rear of their belt.

DATA FILE

MANUFACTURER: Imperial Department of Military Research

CLASS: Military body armor

IMPERVIOUS TO: Projectile weapons and blast shrapnel

RESISTANT TO: Glancing blaster bolts and limited exposure to vacuum of space

Front

Side

Rear

IMPERIAL GROUND VEHICLES

Most worlds happily welcomed the Empire at first. As time went on, however, planets needed more persuasion to remain loyal to the Emperor. The Empire now ensures obedience with its advanced military vehicles.

AT-DP walker

AT-DPs are essentially high-speed tanks on legs, and are one of several walker models used by the Empire. On Lothal they are quite effective at clearing out squatting farmers and other "Loth-rats" when land is needed for new factories.

Imperial Troop Transport

Hovercraft such as the Imperial Troop Transport (ITT) are an ideal way to move soldiers in times of conflict. Likewise, when dangerous prisoners need relocating, ITTs double as dependable prison transports. Ample firepower deters both attackers and would-be escapees.

Imperial speeder bike

For stormtroopers who prefer high speeds, there is no better way to hunt down rebels than on a speeder bike. Their blaster cannons can cut a full-scale revolt down to a minor disturbance from 1000 meters away—a lethal advantage.

AT-DP

AT-DPs (All Terrain Defence Pods) are faster and more durable than the older single-pilot AT-RT series. Their presence patrolling the streets of Lothal is an intimidating sight, meant to discourage rebel uprisings.

DATA FILE

MANUFACTURER: Kuat Drive Yards
CLASS: All Terrain Defence Pod
DIMENSIONS: 6.2 x 7.5 x 11.6 m (20.3 x 24.6 x 38 ft)
ARMAMENT: 1 Kyuzo Maad-38 heavy laser cannon

Rear

Front

Side

Crushing rebellion

Walkers are used by the Imperial Army as a "force-multiplier." They enable a small number of Imperial personnel to patrol large areas and manage crowds with variable levels of force.

Front viewport

Side viewport

Heavy laser cannon

Imperial walkers

AT-DPs are designed for patrols and scouting missions. They can chase suspicious vehicles, but lack the firepower of larger walkers and are used mainly for sentry duty and policing the capital.

Gyro hip-joint system

AT-DP pilots

AT-DPs generally carry two pilots. The pilot seated in front controls navigation, while the pilot behind operates the laser cannon. AT-DP pilots are well-trained and cocky, but as walkers can sometimes stumble, they also wear heavy armor.

Reinforced helmet

Air filtration nozzle

Armored driving gauntlets

Armor-plated boots

"A rogue walker is loose in the Academy!"

COMMANDANT ARESKO

Shock-absorbing hydraulic limbs

Terrain-sensing stabilizer pad

Pilot (for scale)

IMPERIAL TROOP TRANSPORT

Citizens of Lothal stay clear of Imperial Troop Transports when they hear them approaching their neighborhood. It always means one of two things: either stormtroopers are moving in, or Imperials are moving the locals out.

Transparisteel viewport

Forward turret gun

Thick frontal armor

Imperial workhorse

ITTs constantly move troops between important locations. They are one of the military's most dependable vehicles due to their sturdy construction. On Lothal, the Empire also uses these hefty transports to forcibly relocate farmers whose land it has seized.

"Sir, the prisoners are escaping!"

TRANSPORT DRIVER

Dorsal dual heavy laser cannon

DATA FILE

MANUFACTURER: Ubrikkian Industries
CLASS: Imperial Troop Transport
DIMENSIONS: 3.5 x 4.5 x 8.7 m (11.5 x 14.7 x 28.5 ft)
ARMAMENT: 2 forward laser guns, 1 dorsal twin laser turret

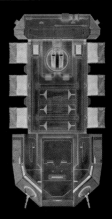

Top

Side

Front

Auto-locking doors

Troop/ prisoner compartment

Access hatch

Covering ground

Speeder bikes are ideal for long-distance scouting missions and patrolling large areas with minimal use of fuel or personnel. More nimble than Troop Transports, they allow stormtroopers to survey difficult terrain or chase after fleeing suspects.

Floodlights

Tilt control handlebar

Engine housing

Stabilizer wings

Air intake cooling vents

Brake pedal

IMPERIAL SPEEDER BIKE

Speeder bikes are indispensible to the Imperial military. They are fitted with a pair of forward blaster cannons, and work alongside AT-DPs and TIE fighters to form a high-speed strike force, cutting down escaping rebels.

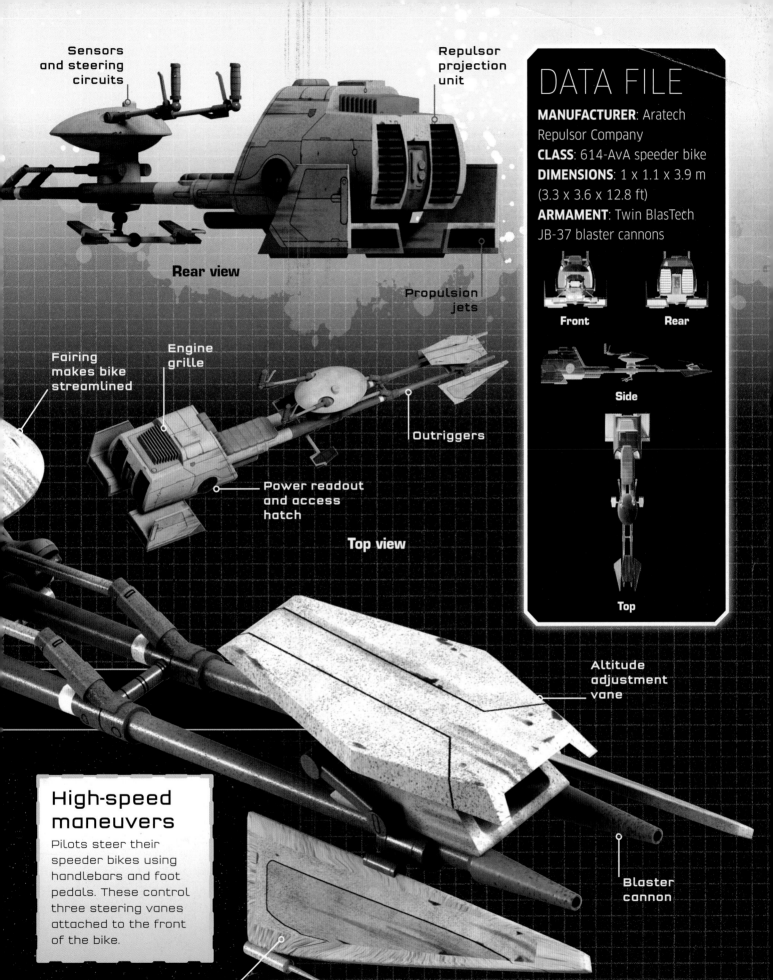

Sensors
and steering
circuits

Repulsor
projection
unit

Rear view

Propulsion
jets

Fairing
makes bike
streamlined

Engine
grille

Outriggers

Power readout
and access
hatch

Top view

DATA FILE

MANUFACTURER: Aratech
Repulsor Company
CLASS: 614-AvA speeder bike
DIMENSIONS: 1 x 1.1 x 3.9 m
(3.3 x 3.6 x 12.8 ft)
ARMAMENT: Twin BlasTech
JB-37 blaster cannons

Front   **Rear**

Side

Top

Altitude
adjustment
vane

Blaster
cannon

High-speed maneuvers

Pilots steer their
speeder bikes using
handlebars and foot
pedals. These control
three steering vanes
attached to the front
of the bike.

Steering vane

IMPERIAL PROPAGANDA

The Imperial Commission for the Preservation of the New Order (COMPNOR) has created an education program to convince citizens of the benefits of life under the rule of the Empire.

False advertising?

Posters and Holonet broadcasts are used to brainwash citizens. The Imperials try to make people believe that they are the heroes who are bringing peace, security, and prosperity to Lothal and the wider galaxy. They claim that the rebels are criminals who bring chaos and instability.

Symbol of the Empire

The Imperial crest is a modified version of the emblem of the Old Republic. It appears on flags, ships, uniforms, and everywhere else that the Empire displays its power.

Empire everywhere

Imperial propaganda posters are on display across Lothal, and all public places must show Imperial broadcasts. The government has also created "Empire Day," a holiday that celebrates the founding of the Empire 14 years ago.

TIE fighters are an iconic symbol of the Empire

Stormtroopers feature heavily in propaganda

Says "Join the Imperial Army"

RECRUITMENT

Stormtrooper recruitment posters are designed to inspire loyalty, but when the Empire doesn't receive enough volunteers, it forces the local population into service.

IMPERIAL NAVY

The Republic Navy was re-organized into the Imperial Navy following the Clone Wars, and now enforces the reign of the Emperor. It fights to strengthen and expand the Empire by protecting Imperial systems and crushing rebellion.

Imperial freighter

Specially constructed Imperial freighters carry supplies to remote outposts and bases. They must be closely guarded to prevent attacks by pirates or rebels.

TIE fighter

TIE fighters are small, fast, easy to maneuver, and are deployed in vast numbers. These one-pilot starfighters are ideal for scouting missions, space combat, and chasing rebel ships.

Star Destroyer

The heart of the Imperial Navy is its fleet of Star Destroyers. Part warship and part gigantic mobile base, they represent the most powerful military force in the galaxy. Most planets surrender rather than face even a single Star Destroyer.

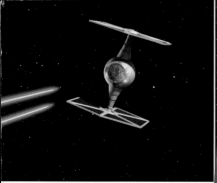

The cockpit

TIE fighter cockpits are cramped. They have to fit in flight controls, targeting systems, view screens, a flight recorder, locator beacon, and a single pilot.

Agile, but fragile

To maximize agility and minimize power demands, TIE fighters lack deflector shields, life support, ejection systems, and hyperdrives. TIE pilots regard these as tools of cowards!

Cockpit access hatch

Wing detachment joint

Main viewport

Low temperature laser tip

Solar array support frame

Solar energy collectors

TIE FIGHTER

TIE fighters are one of the most recognizable symbols of the Imperial Navy's power. Their precision and streamlined design is a point of pride for TIE pilots. New factories have been built on Lothal to mass-produce them.

Flight controls

A TIE fighter's controls are relatively simple. They are so intuitive that Zeb and Ezra are able to work them out on-the-fly when they steal one!

Reinforced
flight helmet

Gas
transfer
hose

DATA FILE

MANUFACTURER: Sienar Fleet Systems

CLASS: Twin Ion Engine starfighter

DIMENSIONS: 6.7 x 7.5 x 5.3 m (22 x 24.6 x 17.4 ft)

ARMAMENT: 2 laser cannons

Front

Rear

Side

"Get your hands off my craft!"

TIE FIGHTER·PILOT

Strength in numbers

As TIE fighters lack shields or armor, they are most effective when attacking in large numbers, enabling them to overwhelm their targets. Each TIE fighter is identical, and TIE pilots may never fly the same craft twice. As a result, they rarely develop emotional ties to their ships.

TIE fighter pilots

Space combat is a disorienting experience. Only 10 percent of cadets in the Imperial pilot training program actually graduate. Pilots are an elite class within the Navy, and tend to be both proud and arrogant.

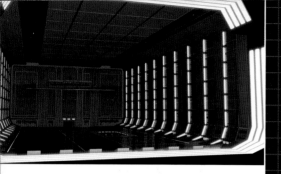

Main hangar

Tractor beams draw disabled ships into the main hangar, where stormtroopers wait to board and capture them. TIE fighters stand ready to launch in nearby hangars.

Targeting array

Shield generator

Main bridge

Primary reactor (at core)

Crew quarters

Heavy turbolaser batteries

Armored hull plating

Lateral quad laser battery

STAR DESTROYER

The Imperial Star Destroyer hovering above Lothal signifies the planet's importance to the Empire, and indicates troubling rebel activity below. Agent Kallus is confident his ship—*Lawbringer*—can handle anything, with its 72 TIE fighters and 9,700 stormtroopers.

The Bridge

High-ranking officers, and occasionally, invited dignitaries, may gaze out of the windows of the bridge. The crew, however, are confined to work stations in pits below.

DATA FILE

MANUFACTURER: Kuat Drive Yards
CLASS: *Imperial I*-class Star Destroyer
DIMENSIONS: 1,600 m (5,249 ft) (length)
ARMAMENT: 60 Taim & Bab XX-9 heavy turbolaser batteries, 60 Borstel NK-7 ion cannons, 10 Phylon 07 tractor beam projectors

Command ships

Imperial commanders use Star Destroyers as their personal bases of operations. Star Destroyers intimidate not only with their size and firepower, but also with the ruthlessness of their commanding officers.

Agent Kallus

Main hangar
(underneath hull)

"I never dreamed the rebels would be foolish enough to attack a Star Destroyer."

AGENT KALLUS

Imperial Symbol

Star Destroyers are a frightening symbol of the Empire's might. A single Star Destroyer can overtake most fleeing ships and overwhelm entire rebellious worlds.

Pursuit tractor beams

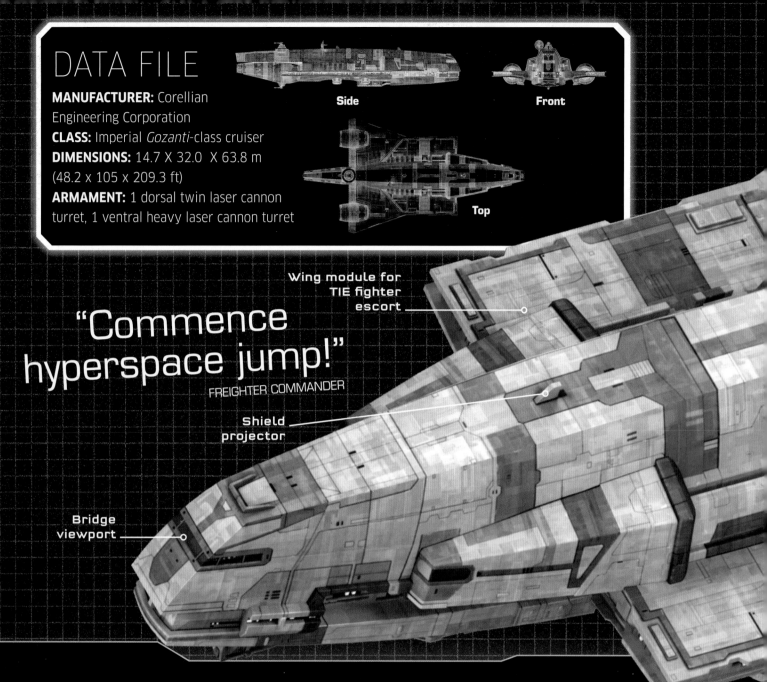

DATA FILE

MANUFACTURER: Corellian Engineering Corporation
CLASS: Imperial *Gozanti*-class cruiser
DIMENSIONS: 14.7 X 32.0 X 63.8 m (48.2 x 105 x 209.3 ft)
ARMAMENT: 1 dorsal twin laser cannon turret, 1 ventral heavy laser cannon turret

Side

Front

Top

Wing module for TIE fighter escort

"Commence hyperspace jump!"

FREIGHTER COMMANDER

Shield projector

Bridge viewport

IMPERIAL FREIGHTER

Gozanti-class cruisers are heavily armored to deter assaults from pirates and other hostile forces. The class is used by many independent factions, but the Imperial version employs heavier shielding, faster engines, and superior weaponry.

Primary
sensor
array

Ion turbine
engine

Twin laser
cannon turret

Hyperdrive

Cell blocks

Freighters have large prison
cells to transport rebel
prisoners, traitors, and other
trouble-makers to Imperial
prisons and labor camps.

Valuable cargoes

Imperial freighters are used to carry
important cargo, such as weapons
and prisoners. To defend these prized
shipments, the transports can carry
their own TIE fighter escorts and a
squad of stormtroopers.

Landing
gear

Loading
elevator

TIE fighter
docking clamp

Ventral
laser turret

Underside view

Commandant Aresko and Taskmaster Grint are commanding officers stationed in Capital City on Lothal. They manage Imperial military operations on the planet while also training cadets at the Imperial Academy.

COMMANDANT ARESKO

Commandant Cumberlayne Aresko is cruel and unsympathetic, both to the citizens of Lothal and the cadets at the Academy. His biggest weakness is overestimating his own abilities and importance.

Imperial code cylinder

FOR THE EMPIRE!

Nothing but service to the Empire would ever appeal to Aresko and Grint. They are wholly devoted to the corrupt Imperial regime, and benefit greatly from it.

DATA FILE

SPECIES: Human
AGE: Late 30s
HOMEWORLD: Unknown
SPECIAL EQUIPMENT:
Blaster pistol

Imperial
officer's disc

TASKMASTER GRINT

Taskmaster Myles Grint is a man of few
words. Aresko does most of the talking
while Grint follows his lead. What he
lacks in intellect however, is made up
for with strength and brutishness.
Grint relies on his size to
intimidate, and on his muscles
to achieve his goals.

Rank insignia
plaque

Officer's tunic

DID YOU KNOW?

The Empire looks
down on aliens, so
it is rare for non-
humans to serve as
Imperial officers.

Belt buckle
with data
storage
compartment

DATA FILE

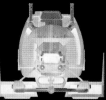

Front

MANUFACTURER: Aratech Repulsor Company
CLASS: 614-AvA speeder bike (customized)
DIMENSIONS: 1 x 1.1 x 3.9 m (3.3 x 3.6 x 12.8 ft)
ARMAMENT: Twin BlasTech JB-37 blaster cannons

Side

Ezra's speeder bike

Ezra drives a surplus Imperial speeder bike, repainted to match his personal tastes and also blend into traffic. He has had limited driving experience, and even less target practice with the blasters of a moving speeder.

Forward fairing (shields sensors and steering)

Outrigger

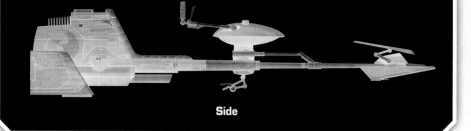

Blaster cannon

Steering vane

REBEL SPEEDER BIKES

Kanan knows from personal experience that being an effective rebel—and staying alive—requires more than just Jedi training. He and Ezra also need to practice driving in hazardous situations.

Kanan's speeder bike

Kanan stores his speeder aboard the *Ghost*, hauling it out for supply runs and missions in Capital City. He and Ezra practice by running an obstacle course as a team, while bull's-eyeing a few Loth-rats, too.

Moll K-19 power generator

Acceleration pedal

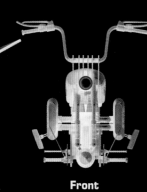

Front

¾ view

DATA FILE

MANUFACTURER: Zebulon Dak Speeder Corporation
CLASS: Joben T-85 speeder bike
DIMENSIONS: 1.03 x 1.04 x 2.34 m (3.3 x 3.4 x 7.7 ft)
ARMAMENT: Dusat aft-firing EMP emitter (disabled)

Combat maneuvers

Hera is a clever navigator and one of the best star-pilots this side of the galaxy. She handles the ship's controls better than anyone on board, managing to hold off incoming fighters while Kanan and the crew shoot them down.

DOGFIGHT!

The *Ghost* is usually successful at evading Imperial sensors, but she cannot always remain undetected. Dogfights are unavoidable when tangling with the Empire. Fortunately for the rebels, skilled pilot Hera is at the *Ghost*'s controls!

TIE attacks

Imperial ships come in fast but their pilots are too cocky. Now that the Empire is the dominant power in space, TIE pilots don't get much practice, so they tend to underestimate their targets.

Target destroyed

Without deflector shields, TIE fighters don't hold together when hit by the *Ghost's* main guns. No matter how many ships the rebels seem to destroy though, the TIEs just keep on coming.

AGENT KALLUS

When the rebels' activities on Lothal begin to attract attention, Agent Kallus of the Imperial Security Bureau is sent to stop them. With all Imperial forces on Lothal at his personal disposal, he is a powerful opponent.

RUTHLESS ENEMY

Like all ISB agents, Kallus exhibits an unwavering sense of duty to the Emperor. He loathes disorder and detests rebellion. His inflated ego and sense of superiority add to his hatred of the lawless outer frontier.

Bayonet

Folding stock

Folding pistol-grip handle

Blaster barrel

Kallus's helmet

The helmet that Kallus wears symbolizes his status as an ISB agent. It is designed for use in riot control and heavy combat situations. The sight of helmeted ISB agents is intimidating enough to deter most civilian protests.

Lasan bo-rifle

Kallus has undergone extensive training, and is lethal in hand-to-hand combat. He took part in the destruction of Zeb's homeworld of Lasan, and took his signature Lasan bo-rifle from there. It is a trophy from a fallen Lasat Honor Guard whom he defeated in battle.

ISB helmet

Combat
armor

THE IMPERIAL
SECURITY BUREAU

Kallus is a member of the
Imperial Security Bureau (ISB),
the secret police who monitor
loyalty to the Empire. ISB agents
investigate signs of rebellion
and brutally crush them
wherever they are found.

DID YOU KNOW?

Kallus's Imperial
code name is
"ISB-021." The low
number indicates
his senior rank.

Electromagnetic
pulse-generator tip

"It's over for you, Jedi!"

Agent Kallus

CIKATRO VIZAGO

The devious Devaronian Cikatro Vizago is the chief scoundrel of the Lothal underground. The rebels have to pay the bills somehow, which occasionally means smuggling stolen goods or running errands for Vizago.

FRIEND OR FOE?

Vizago only really cares about money. According to Hera, "He'd sell his mother to Jawas for a couple of credits." Nobody aboard the *Ghost* trusts him, but they rely on him for information and funding.

LOTHAL KINGPIN

As head of the Broken Horn crime syndicate, Cikatro Vizago is a source of valuable information. In exchange for a shipment of blasters stolen from the Empire, for example, Vizago tells the rebel crew the whereabouts of some important Wookiee prisoners.

Power cartridge release

Sight adapter

Barrel adapter

Barrel shroud with cooling vents

Pressure-sensitive trigger

Power gauge

Weighted, ribbed handle

Side view

Vizago's Blaster

Vizago carries a popular "Vilmarh's Revenge" blaster pistol, manufactured by DevTech Sidearms. The versatile model is easily customized via adapters, and its rate of fire is increased with added trigger pressure.

Rear view

Male horns
(females are
hornless)

Lethal
spiked
gloves

Valuable
earrings

Long,
pointed ears

Strong
Devaronian
build

DATA FILE

SPECIES: Devaronian
AGE: 40
HOMEWORLD: Devaron
SPECIAL EQUIPMENT: Vilmarh's
Revenge blaster, the *Broken Horn*
ship, IG-RM droids

VIZAGO'S GANG

Cikatro Vizago's Broken Horn Syndicate is a criminal organization dealing in stolen Imperial weapons and other black market goods. His organization spans several planetary systems, but the Lothal underworld is his home turf.

Loading elevator

IG-RM thug droids

Vizago uses a crew of IG-RM thug droids, armed with BlasTech DLT-18 laser rifles, to do his dirty work. These nasty IG droids were developed by Holowan Laboratories, creators of the IG-86 sentinel droid line (also popular with gangsters) and the IG-100 MagnaGuards (a favorite of the late General Grievous).

"Business is all that matters."

CIKATRO VIZAGO

Cargo
containers

Ion turbine
engines

Broken Horn (docked)

The *Broken Horn*

The *Broken Horn* is Vizago's personal transportation and
flagship. The vessel is a modified C-ROC *Gozanti*-class cruiser,
manufactured by the Corellian Engineering Corp. At more
than 70 meters (230 feet) long, it has ample cargo holds for
illegal goods. The *Broken Horn* has few weapons though,
so Vizago depends on its heavy shields and powerful
engines to make quick escapes.

Bridge

Broken Horn (flight mode)

Communications dish

Fires ionized
plasma

Disruptors

Vizago uses the rebels to steal a
shipment of T-7 disruptors. These
powerful weapons are designed to
disable starships, but can also be used
on living beings—with gruesome results.

Large stock
to absorb
heavy recoil

Power
cell

T-7 Ion Disruptor

SABINE THE ARTIST

Sabine's clothes are often splattered paint from sudden bursts of artistic inspiration. She adds color to the live the rebels in many ways, and is resp for the team's inventive calling cards

PERSONAL TOUCHES

Sabine enjoys customizing the rebels' gear, and leaving her mark on the *Ghost*, too. Her room is decorated with pictures of bounty hunters Cad Bane and Embo, sketches of Lothal animals, and lots of anti-stormtrooper symbols.

BURSTING WITH CREATIVITY

The two things Sabine seems to love most—art and blowing things up—are even better when combined. Sabine's explosives are always identified by her signature artistic flair: bright colors and starbird shapes.

PAINT THE TOWN

Sabine's airbrushes are among her most prized possessions. She is always ready to customize her mission objectives with a splash of color... and the armor of an unconscious stormtrooper is an irresistible blank canvas!

Starships

Tiny TIE fighters threaten by attacking in huge swarms, while Star Destroyers are the titans of the galaxy. These giant vessels defeat ships by either blasting them into dust or by swallowing them whole using tractor beams.

Broken Horn transport
Length: 72.8 m

Imperial freighter
Length: 63.8 m

Ghost
Length: 43.9 m

TIE fighter
Length: 5.3 m

HOW BIG?

Ground vehicles

Weight isn't an issue for vehicles fitted with repulsorlifts, such as Troop Transports and speeder bikes. On the other hand, walkers use weight to their advantage in order to gain momentum. They can even crush enemies underfoot.

Imperial speeder bike
Weight: 120 kg

Kanan's speeder bike
Weight: 160 kg

AT-DP
Weight: 11,200 kg

Imperial Troop Transport
Weight: 20,600 kg

Imperial Star Destroyer
Length: 1,600 m

Size matters not for Jedi, but when physical force is required, military power is measured by strength and bulk. The Empire tries to overwhelm its enemies with numbers and size, but the rebels fight back with resourcefulness.

Humans and aliens

Pau'ans and Lasat may be bigger and stronger than humans and Twi'leks... but through the Force, even the smallest beings have the potential to become great heroes.

Zeb	Kanan	Hera	Sabine	Ezra	Chopper	The Inquisitor
Height: 2.1 m	Height: 1.9 m	Height: 1.8 m	Height: 1.7 m	Height: 1.6 m	Height: 1 m	Height: 2.0 m

WULLFFWARRO AND KITWARR

The Empire conquered the Wookiee world of Kashyyyk and enslaved the population. Wullffwarro is the noble leader of a group of Wookiees taken prisoner by the Empire, alongside his young son, Kitwarr.

Strong shoulders from climbing giant trees

Long male beard

Traditional Wookiee arm band

ENEMY OF EMPIRE

Wullffwarro once fought for the Republic, and now he helps the rebels. Wookiees are brave warriors who have saved the lives of many a human, Twi'lek, and Lasat, though the Empire views them as beasts.

FROM HERO TO SLAVE

Wullffwarro's Wookiees are sent to the spice mines of Kessel to work as slave labor. The Wookiees had always lived in the lush forests of Kashyyyk, so the harsh conditions in the mines will not suit them at all.

Youthful light-colored fur

BRIGHT-EYED INNOCENCE

The rebels attempt a dangerous rescue mission to save Wullffwarro and Kitwarr, along with the other Wookiees. Little Kitwarr is terrified when he is thrown into the middle of the conflict that results.

Small hands not yet trained for battle

Wullffwarro

Kitwarr

DATA FILE

SPECIES: Wookiee
AGE: Unknown
HOMEWORLD: Kashyyyk
SPECIAL EQUIPMENT: None

WOOKIEE GUNSHIP

Since the Empire invaded Kashyyyk, those left in the Wookiee military must now focus their efforts on battling slavery. Wookiee gunships, custom-painted in traditional clan designs, are sent on assault and rescue missions.

DATA FILE

MANUFACTURER: Appazanna Engineering Works
CLASS: *Auzituck* anti-slaver gunship
DIMENSIONS: 6.0 x 7.6 x 14.7 m (19.7 x 24.9 x 48.2 ft)
ARMAMENT: 3 Sureggi twin laser cannons in pod mountings

¾ view

Front

Primary pilot cockpit

Traditional Wookiee bracelet

Shaggy, water-resistant fur

Wookiee warriors

Wookiees are brave warriors who fought for the Republic during the Clone Wars. They defended their homeworld of Kashyyyk and fought for the freedom of other systems as well. But when Kashyyyk was conquered by the Empire, many Wookiees were taken as slaves.

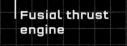

Dorsal laser cannons

Fusial thrust engine

Concentrated firepower

The ship's rapid-fire Sureggi laser cannons are all forward-facing, making a head-on confrontation with a Wookiee gunship a no-win scenario.

Repulsorlift stabilizers

Appazanna Engineering Works

On Kashyyyk, Appazanna Engineering built ships with indigenous Wookiee design features. As well as the gunship, their other well-known craft included the *Oevvaor* catamaran and *Raddaugh Gnasp* fluttercraft.

SPICE MINES OF KESSEL

The barren mines of Kessel are one of the most feared labor camps in the galaxy. A group of Wookiees, including Wullffwarro and his son Kitwarr, are sent to the planet by Agent Kallus.

Mining world

The royal family of Kessel allows the harvesting of spice on one hemisphere of their world. They turn a blind eye to the brutal working conditions and the transformation of the medicinal spice mineral into a dangerous drug.

Spice mines J-1 through J-99

Spice mines L-1 through L-99

Border of spice operations

Lush sanctuaries ruled by Kessel royal family

Exposed rock layers

Active mine entrance

Observation platform

Spice sifting mills

Landing platforms

Spice refining tanks

Slave workforce

Spice mining is incredibly dangerous, so the Empire uses slave labor. Prisoners are sent to Kessel in order to make them disappear permanently. Many Wookiees have spent their final days digging in the dreary mines.

MINING OPERATIONS

On Kessel, spice mining is on an industrial scale. Deep pits, mine shafts, and massive refineries cover the surface. Several other systems around the galaxy support spice mining too, including Ryloth and Naboo. The Pyke Syndicate is one of the largest dealers in illegal spice.

"It's a death sentence."

HERA SYNDULLA

Painted
cadet helmet

Unconventional
lightsaber
design

Unlikely Padawan

Ezra is eager for the approval of his new mentor, but he often misunderstands Kanan's hesitation, and is easily offended by his comments. Ezra's sensitivity can be both a strength and weakness.

Hand in
"Force push"
position

Belt holds
lightsaber

EZRA'S JEDI TRAINING

Jedi Padawans (apprentices) spend years learning from their Masters. Jedi training includes tough physical and mental exercises, and a final series of perilous trials. Ezra's training has only just begun.

Wary mentor

Kanan would prefer to find a more qualified Jedi Master to mentor Ezra, but few remain. He resolves to train Ezra wholeheartedly, and not merely "try."

Protective gloves allow easy movement

Jedi use the Force to persuade the weak-minded

Close-fitting clothes suit lightsaber combat

Using the Force

Jedi use the Force to help others and defend themselves. They may move or levitate objects, perform impossible acrobatics, and sense danger or even other Force-users nearby.

R2-D2 AND C-3PO

These two droids have played vital roles in recent galactic history. Their personalities could not be more different, but somehow they always stick together. Now they have been given a new mission: helping to negotiate an Imperial arms deal. On this mission they meet some of the rebels.

A FIESTY LITTLE ONE

R2-D2 is underappreciated and underestimated by C-3PO, who would be entirely lost without him. R2's handy gadgets and independent thinking continue to get the two out of trouble, as R2-D2 makes the most of bad situations.

Primary photoreceptor

Retractable arm covers

DATA FILE

CLASS: Astromech droid
MANUFACTURER: Industrial Automation
HOMEWORLD: Naboo
EQUIPMENT: Grasping arm, computer probe, booster rockets, scanner antennae, holographic projector

Rocket booster system

DID YOU KNOW?

C-3PO and R2-D2 first met on the planet Tatooine, nearly 30 years ago.

Retractable third tread

DATA FILE

CLASS: Protocol droid
MANUFACTURER: Cybot Galactica (assembled by Anakin Skywalker)
HOMEWORLD: Tatooine
EQUIPMENT: TranLang III communication module

Photoreceptors with Myriad Visual System

Gold chromium finish

Primary power coupler outlet

CLEVER DROID

Fluent in over six million forms of communication, C-3PO is the perfect translator for diplomatic missions, but somehow he always finds himself in trouble. His memory was deleted at the end of the Clone Wars, which keeps his focus on the task in hand.

Reinforced knee joint

Salvaged shin plate

Bail Organa

Senator Organa owns C-3PO and R2-D2. He loans them to Imperial Governor Pryce on Lothal, which leads to an unexpected adventure for the pair.

THEIR LOT IN LIFE

The fate of R2-D2 and C-3PO is dictated by galactic circumstances beyond their control. Now owned by a secretly rebellious senator, they remain loyal to their new master.

THE INQUISITOR

The Inquistor is an evil, shadowy menace with a single purpose: to hunt down and destroy Jedi. He uses the dark side to turn his targets' inner secrets against them, but his most dangerous weapon is his cold, calculating mind.

Master of fear

Like all Pau'ans, the Inquisitor prefers to dwell in darkness rather than light. Sinister red tattoos cover his furrowed head, striking fear into his suspects. Fear is his most powerful tool in his interrogations of Force-sensitive beings.

SERVANT OF THE DARK SIDE

The Inquisitor has been ordered by Darth Vader to hunt down the remaining Jedi. He exists only to serve the dark side and the Emperor. His mission is to pass judgment on Force-users, and he shows his victims no mercy.

Red dark-side blade

Access hatch

Laser tip

High-performance solar array

TIE Advanced

Due to the sensitive nature of the Inquisitor's top-secret missions, he has been entrusted with an experimental TIE Advanced v1 prototype. The ship is fitted with a hyperdrive and basic shields.

DID YOU KNOW?

Pau'ans prefer a diet of raw meat, which they chew using their sharp upper teeth.

DATA FILE

SPECIES: Pau'an
AGE: Mid-40s (human equivalent)
HOMEWORLD: Utapau
EQUIPMENT: Double-bladed
lightsaber, helmet, TIE
Advanced v1

Protective
collar

Imperial
insignia

Electronic
controls

Dark-side
tattoos

JEDI HUNTER

The Inquisitor uses the dark side
of the Force, but he is not a Sith.
The highly intelligent Inquisitor
has been trained not only to
identify Jedi, but also to analyze
their fighting styles, capabilities,
and the Jedi traditions they
follow. He is even able to
identify a Jedi's mentor.

"The Jedi are dead, but there is another path."
The Inquisitor

HE INQUISITOR'S IGHTSABER

a servant of the dark side, the Inquisitor uses ightsaber not to defend, but to destroy his mies without mercy. His weapon is elegantly igned to end battles quickly, efficiently, and a minimum of effort.

A skilled executioner

The Inquisitor's fighting style and spinning lightsaber are meant to unnerve his enemies. Fear causes an inexperienced Jedi to become unbalanced and sloppy, which makes them vulnerable to a deadly strike.

DATA FILE

MANUFACTURER: Unknown
MODEL: Double-bladed spinning lightsaber
FEATURES: Double and single (crescent) blade modes, spinning double-blade mode

Crescent mode

Double-blade mode

A new weapon

The Inquisitor's unique lightsaber design has several modes. The crescent-mode is a single-bladed lightsaber. In disc-mode, a second blade is drawn. Both blades can then spin around the disc, forming a terrifying wall of energy! The Inquisitor holds the lightsaber in one hand, or throws it at his opponents.

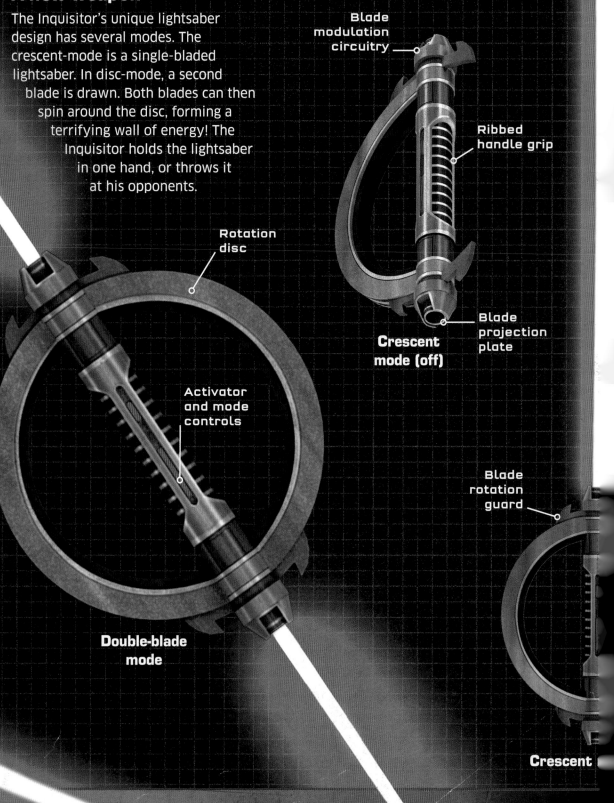

Blade
modulation
circuitry

Ribbed
handle grip

Blade
projection
plate

**Crescent
mode (off)**

Rotation
disc

Activator
and mode
controls

**Double-blade
mode**

Blade
rotation
guard

Crescent

KANAN VS THE INQUISITOR

The rebels learn that a surviving Jedi Master is being held in a remote prison by the Empire. They do not realize that the Inquisitor also waits for them at the prison, with a single mission—to finish off the last of the Jedi...

Jedi usually use blue or green crystals for their lightsabers

Aggressive attack stance

Sith and dark side users carry red lightsabers

Sinister encounter

When Kanan first battles the Inquisitor, he quickly realizes that this enemy is more than a match for his incomplete Jedi training. However, he must fight to hold the Inquisitor off so that the other rebels can escape.

"The Spire" is a remote Imperial facility located in the cold mountains of Stygeon Prime. The impregnable prison is blast-proof, ray-shielded, and protected by anti-ship weapons, TIE fighters, and of course, stormtroopers.

Defensive Jedi posture

"I'm not making deals with you."

KANAN JARRUS

LOTHAL'S ACADEMY FOR YOUNG IMPERIALS

Lothal's Imperial Academy trains the next generation of men and women for service to the Emperor. Commandant Aresko and Taskmaster Grint are the unforgiving instructors here. Ezra must infiltrate the Academy on a risky mission.

Each cadet has own color

Ezra's mission

Ezra sneaks into Lothal's Imperial Academy and poses as a cadet in order to steal an Imperial decoder. In the process he learns that the Inquisitor intends to take fellow cadet Jai Kell as his prisoner. Ezra enlists his friend Zare Leonis to help them escape.

Zare Leonis

Ezra Bridger

Walking out

Zare proves himself a valuable friend and surprising ally. He and Jai hijack an Imperial walker and fight their way out of the Academy. Jai and Ezra escape but Zare chooses to remain behind.

Imperial insignia

Cadet helmet

THE INSIDE MAN

Zare Leonis is a skilled cadet, and incredibly brave. His sister, Dhara, was the star cadet at the Imperial Academy, but she mysteriously vanished. Zare was told that she ran away, but he believes that the Inquisitor may have something to do with her disappearance. He remains at the Academy hoping that he may eventually discover her fate.

Air supply nozzle

DID YOU KNOW?

Zare becomes a spy for the rebels, giving them inside information about Imperial Command.

Smart white cadet uniform

ZARE LEONIS

Protective boots

"We're a crew. A team. In some ways, a family."

Sabine

"Next time they make a move, we'll be waiting for them..."

Agent Kallus

The team at Lucasfilm share how they designed and created *Star Wars Rebels*, how it was influenced by the original film, *Star Wars: A New Hope*, and the inspiration of the concept artist Ralph McQuarrie.

CONTENTS

The *Rebels* interviews

Dave Filoni

A key figure in Lucasfilm Animation, Dave Filoni served as supervising director for *Star Wars: The Clone Wars*, and is now executive producer on *Star Wars Rebels*. Dave is also known for his work on *King of the Hill* and *Avatar: The Last Airbender*.

Joel Aron

Joel Aron has served as CG supervisor on both *The Clone Wars* and *Rebels*. He has also worked in visual effects at Industrial Light & Magic, contributing to *Star Wars*: Episode III *Revenge of the Sith*, and *Indiana Jones and the Kingdom of the Crystal Skull*.

Simon Kinberg

Executive producer Simon Kinberg has worked as a writer and producer on blockbuster movies such as *Mr. and Mrs. Smith*, *Jumper*, *X-Men: First Class*, and *X-Men: Days of Future Past*, as well as *The Fantastic Four* (2015) and *X-Men Apocalypse* (2016).

Concept art of Capital City

INSPIRING REBELS

When designing the characters, worlds, and vehicles of *Rebels,* the production team was determined to match it to the look of the original *Star Wars* trilogy. To accomplish this, they often used existing concept material for inspiration.

Zeb character design from *Rebels*

Concept artist Ralph McQuarrie

Original design for Chewbacca

Ralph McQuarrie

"What I think makes *Rebels* unique is the influence of [concept artist] Ralph McQuarrie. His brush stroke, his color pallet, and sense of pencil lines are what we kind of wanted to have all over this thing. Zeb is like an original McQuarrie Chewbacca, just painted like a purple tiger!"
—Dave Filoni

Ralph McQuarrie's concept art for Episode IV

McQuarrie R2-D2 concept for Episode IV

Articulating arm

Chopper

"There's an obvious reference to Artoo-Detoo in his design. But Ralph's original art for Artoo had those articulating arms. So we were inspired and ran with that. He's like the anti-Artoo and a pain in the butt, sort of selfish and like a house cat."
—Simon Kinberg

"Chopper" from *Rebels*

McQuarrie's concept art of Sicemon, an unused grassland planet for Episode VI

Lothal origins

"Where Ezra lives, where we meet him, the prairie that he lives on, the city, the town that it's adjacent to—all of that, literally down to what the alleys look like in the town—was inspired by Ralph's original art."

—Simon Kinberg

Lothal concept art from *Rebels*

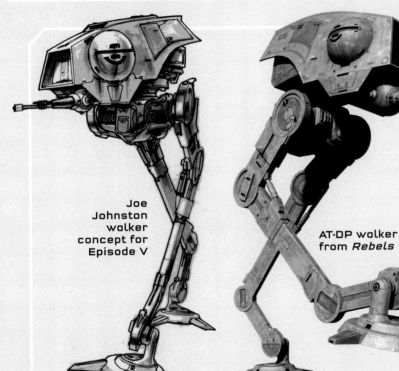

Joe Johnston walker concept for Episode V

AT-DP walker from *Rebels*

Concept artist Joe Johnston

The AT-DP

"There's clearly some influence from concept artist Joe Johnston as well, in our walker. Ours is actually one that Joe had designed for the Episode V scout walker, an abandoned design."

—Dave Filoni

Other influences

"If you look through a lot of discarded work that had been done [for the original trilogy], or things that had just never quite hit the screen, there are always influences that we've really tried to keep."

—Dave Filoni

Imperial speeder bike from *Rebels*

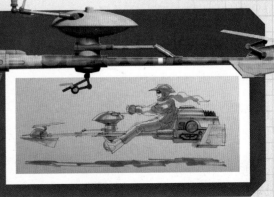

Joe Johnston speeder bike concept for Episode VI

CHARACTER DESIGN

The most important part of creating *Rebels* was the design of the main characters. The rebel crew had to be endearing, while making something new and exciting was also important, especially with the Inquistor.

Taylor Gray—the voice of Ezra

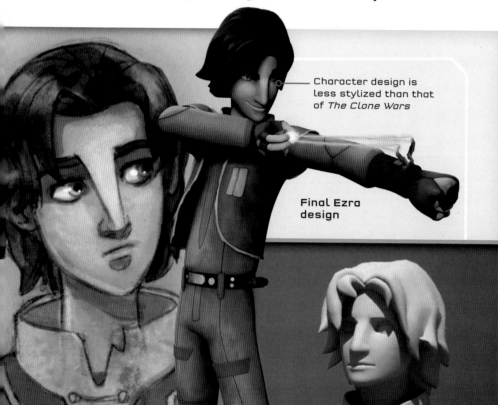

Character design is less stylized than that of *The Clone Wars*

Final Ezra design

Ezra concept art

Ezra pre-texture animation

Ezra clay maquette

Ezra's look

"I would have to look through my pile of sketches to be sure, but I think that I started with Ezra. I remember designing him specifically, and what his look was gonna be. He's actually a little bit 'Karate Kid.' People say 'Aladdin' as well—that's fine, too."

—Dave Filoni

Ezra's voice

"The hardest character to cast was probably Ezra. He was going to have to be authentic and carry the show in a lot of ways. But Taylor [Gray] does a magnificent job with that. He adds a lot of vulnerability, a lot of range, and a lot of likeability to it."

—Dave Filoni

Storyboard panel

Ezra's storyline

"I've been surprised by how Ezra's story has evolved—how we were originally going to treat his parents and his history in the first season, and how we deviated a little bit from that. We thought it would be more interesting to go in a different direction."

—Simon Kinberg

Hera

Hera character concepts

Final design for Hera

"Hera didn't start out as a Twi'lek. She started out as a kind of a short, matronly woman, and then developed into the rather tall, slender-figured woman that you see as a Twi'lek. I knew I didn't want her to be like a 'dancing girl' Twi'lek. I wanted her to be tougher and very assertive."

—Dave Filoni

The Inquisitor

Final Inquisitor design

"It was quite a discussion in Lucasfilm as to who this new villain would be. We tried several different Inquisitors and in the end the Pau'an won out. I think he's got a natural creepy sense to him, with the teeth and the elongated head!"

—Dave Filoni

Creating a unique villain

"How do you position a villain, and make them unique? I think that it's the Inquisitor's analytic attitude: he's very cold, he's very questioning, he's just sucking information out of you. He's a hunter, so we wanted somebody strikingly different."

—Dave Filoni

Used for 3D modeling

The Inquisitor's look

"You know when you look at him that he's not Maul. You know he's not Ventress. You know that he's not Dooku. There's an elegance to his armor, there's an elegance to his movement. He comes across as an educated, sophisticated villain, which I think is always very dangerous."

—Dave Filoni

Inquisitor clay maquette

MAKING REBELS

A single episode of *Rebels* can take months to create. Producing the show takes a skilled team made up of writers, concept artists, matte painters, animators, and lighting and effects experts.

The *Rebels* team reviewing concept art

Visualizing

"Dave will often just come in and say 'Hey, I just saw this thing,' or he'll draw something on my white board, and it's my job to make it come alive. That's a lot of my day, Dave walking into my office like that!"
–Joel Aron

Concept art of Capital City on Lothal

Storyboarding

"As soon as Dave started boarding, he cut actual shots from *A New Hope* into it. It's the same with anything–when we are inside a TIE fighter, when we are inside the *Ghost* cockpit–we try and use the same configurations for the shots as in *A New Hope,* just to get that same feel."
–Joel Aron

Episode set out shot-by-shot

Storyboarding an episode

Colors used as guide for final render

Storyboard concept painting

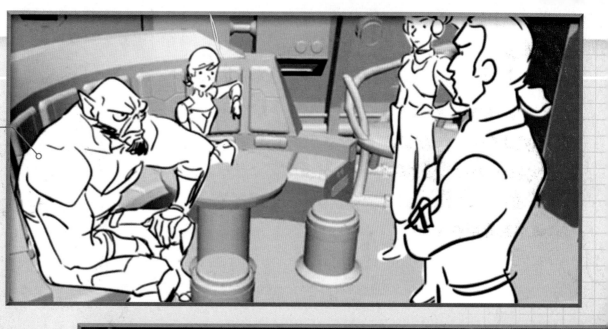

2D placeholders put onto 3D background

Scene mock-up

Character rendering

"I had to think about how our characters would look, being translated from the Ralph McQuarrie-type designs that the team were coming up with. So one of my first roles was initially to come up with how they would render: their look on screen and the shading of their skin."

–Joel Aron

Low-resolution initial 3D render

Effects concept painting

Final frame showing effect

Effects design

"I work with the team to come up with and develop the effects for the show. I go in and paint the look of the effect, and then make that painting 'come alive,' as opposed to just letting software do its thing to make it look like CGI. I want everything to look painted."

–Joel Aron

LONDON, NEW YORK,
MELBOURNE, MUNICH, AND DELHI

For Dorling Kindersley
Senior Editor Sadie Smith
Editor David Fentiman
Senior Art Editor Clive Savage
Designed by Anna Formanek,
Chris Gould, Toby Truphet
Pre-Production Producer Siu Yin Chan
Senior Producer Alex Bell
Managing Editor Laura Gilbert
Managing Art Editor Maxine Pedliham
Publishing Manager Julie Ferris
Art Director Lisa Lanzarini
Publishing Director Simon Beecroft

For Lucasfilm
Executive Editor Jonathan W. Rinzler
Art Director Troy Alders
Story Group Pablo Hidalgo, Leland Chee
Director of Publishing Carol Roeder

First published in the United States
in 2014 by DK Publishing, 4th Floor,
345 Hudson Street, New York, New York 10014

Published in Great Britain by
Dorling Kindersley Limited

A catalog record for this book is available
from the Library of Congress.

DK books are available at special discounts when
purchased in bulk for sales promotions, premiums,
fund-raising, or educational use. For details, contact:
DK Publishing Special Markets,
345 Hudson Street, New York, New York 10014
SpecialSales@dk.com

ISBN: 978-1-4654-2080-0

Color reproduction by Alta Image, UK
Printed and bound by Hung Hing, China

Discover more at **www.dk.com**
Visit the official *Star Wars* website: **www.starwars.com**

With special thanks to author Adam Bray for conducting
the interviews with Lucasfilm, also to Dave Filoni, Simon
Kinberg, and Joel Aron for kindly agreeing to be interviewed,
Tracy Cannobio for arranging the interviews, and Pablo
Hidalgo of Story Group.